I WANT TO KNOW...

?

Which foods are healthy?

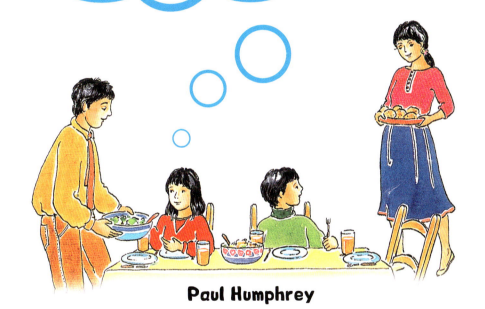

Paul Humphrey

Illustrated by Kareen Taylerson

First published in this edition in 2011 by
Evans Publishing Group
2A Portman Mansions
Chiltern Street
London W1U 6NR

www.evansbooks.co.uk

British Library Cataloguing in Publication Data:
A CIP catalogue record for this book is available from the British Library

ISBN: 9780237544966

Planned and produced by Discovery Books
Cover designed by Rebecca Fox

For permission to reproduce copyright material the author and publishers gratefully
acknowledge the following: Alex Ramsay: page 23, 25; Eye Ubiquitous: page 13;
Image Bank: page 19, 25; istock: cover, page 10, 21, 27 Robert Harding: page 21;
Tony Stone: page 6-7, 9; Zefa: page 15.

Printed by Great Wall Printing Company in Chai Wan, Hong Kong,
August 2011, Job Number 1672.

CONTENTS

4

No, you shouldn't eat too many biscuits.

Biscuits and sweets contain lots of sugar and fat. It is not good for you to eat too many sweet things.

If you help me make dinner I will show you.

To be healthy you should eat the right amount of all kinds of food. This is called a balanced diet.

8

Foods that contain carbohydrates help to give you energy.

Without energy you wouldn't be able to run around and play your favourite sports.

Your body also needs protein. This is found in fish, meat and nuts.

Protein helps to build strong muscles. Can you spot the cashew nuts in this stir fry?

12

Vitamins help to make your body work properly and keep you fit and healthy. Fruit salad gives you lots of vitamins!

Some food is grown in this country and some comes from other countries. It is brought to shops in lorries, by ship, by train and by plane.

Labels on packets and tins
show which country the food
comes from.

18

Wheat is grown in lots of countries. It is harvested in late summer and the wheat seeds are ground into flour.

20

Rice is grown in places where it is warm and wet. Most rice is grown in flooded fields called paddies. There are more than 40,000 different kinds of rice.

22

Fresh milk can turn sour very quickly, so shops sell milk that has been produced in this country. This means it does not have to travel too far before we drink it.

Some milk is made into butter, cheese and yoghurt. These are called dairy products.

24

Tinned and frozen fish comes from different countries all over the world.

You must be careful to buy fish that has been fished sustainably, because many fish are in danger of becoming extinct.

There are many different kinds of fruits. In the summer, many fresh fruits and vegetables can be grown near to where you live. In the winter they may have to be shipped from warmer places.

There are many different kinds of food. Your body needs a good balanced diet so that you can keep fit and healthy.

Fun activities

Can you remember the answers to these questions? Look back through the book to help you. The answers are at the bottom of page 31, but don't peep until you've tried yourself.

1) Why shouldn't you eat too many cakes, biscuits and sweets?
2) Rice is grown in fields called _____.
3) Name three things that milk can be turned into.
4) Look at the pictures below: where do these different foods come from?

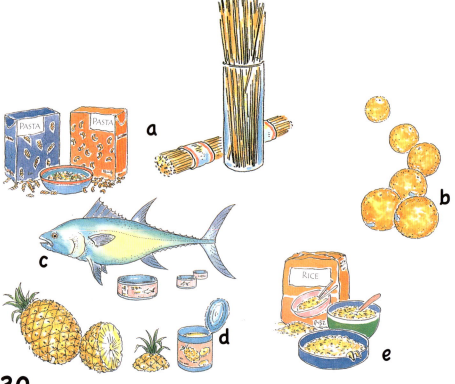

Can you find food in your kitchen that has travelled far?

Look carefully at tins and packets to see where the food has come from. Can you find these places on a map? Which food has travelled the furthest?

Imagine that you have bought a pineapple from the supermarket.

But this pineapple is a magic pineapple that can speak! It tells you all about its journey from Kenya to your kitchen. Write a story describing its journey. Did it grow in a hot or cold climate? How did it travel across the world? How did it get to the supermarket? What was it like to sit on a supermarket shelf?

Interesting websites:

Look at some pictures of where your food comes from:
http://kids.direct.gov.uk/resource_areas/html/Slideshow/27

Learn about different food groups and eating healthily:
http://www.childrenfirst.nhs.uk/kids/health/eat_smart/food_science/index.html

Here you will find ideas for healthy treats:
http//www.bam.gov/sub_foodnutrition/cooltreats.html

Index